Dinosaur Coloring Book To Make You Roar!

Steve Sure

ENJOY

Dinosaur Coloring Book To Make You Roar! One of the year's best coloring books for children (and adults young at heart). Containing 36 amazing images for you to show your artistic skills and includes all popular dinosaurs including the mighty T-Rex, Triceratops, Stegosaurus and Diplodocus along with many more. Each picture is on a separate page so you can cut it out and display your artistic skills.

FREE Dinosaur Masks - Plus there are further 6 free dinosaur masks for you to color and then cut out and have awesome fun with.

Plus you can join our free club and we'll send you all the images as .pdf's so you can print and color them as many times as you wish (including the mask designs). Never run out of a dinosaur coloring picture again!

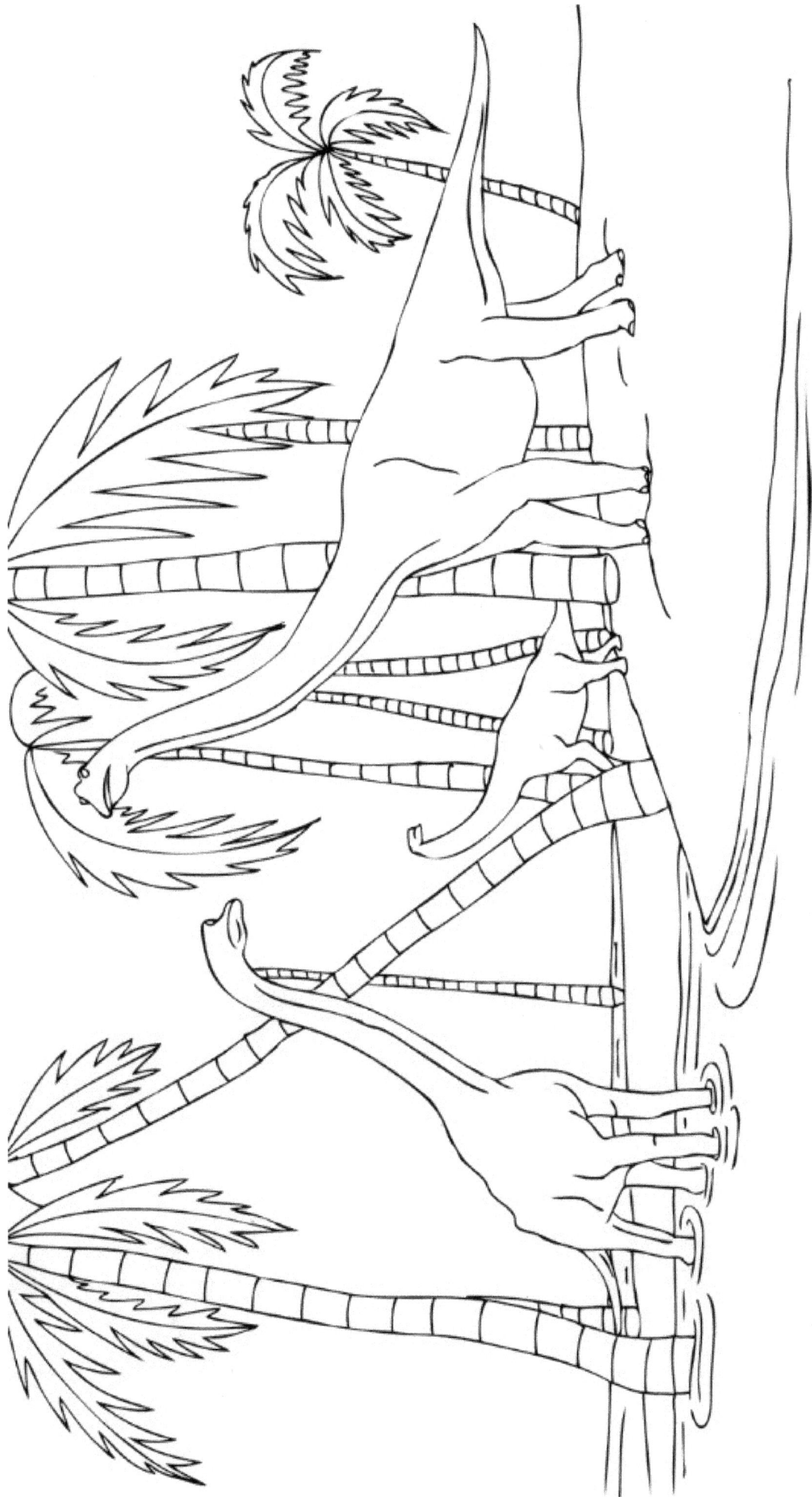

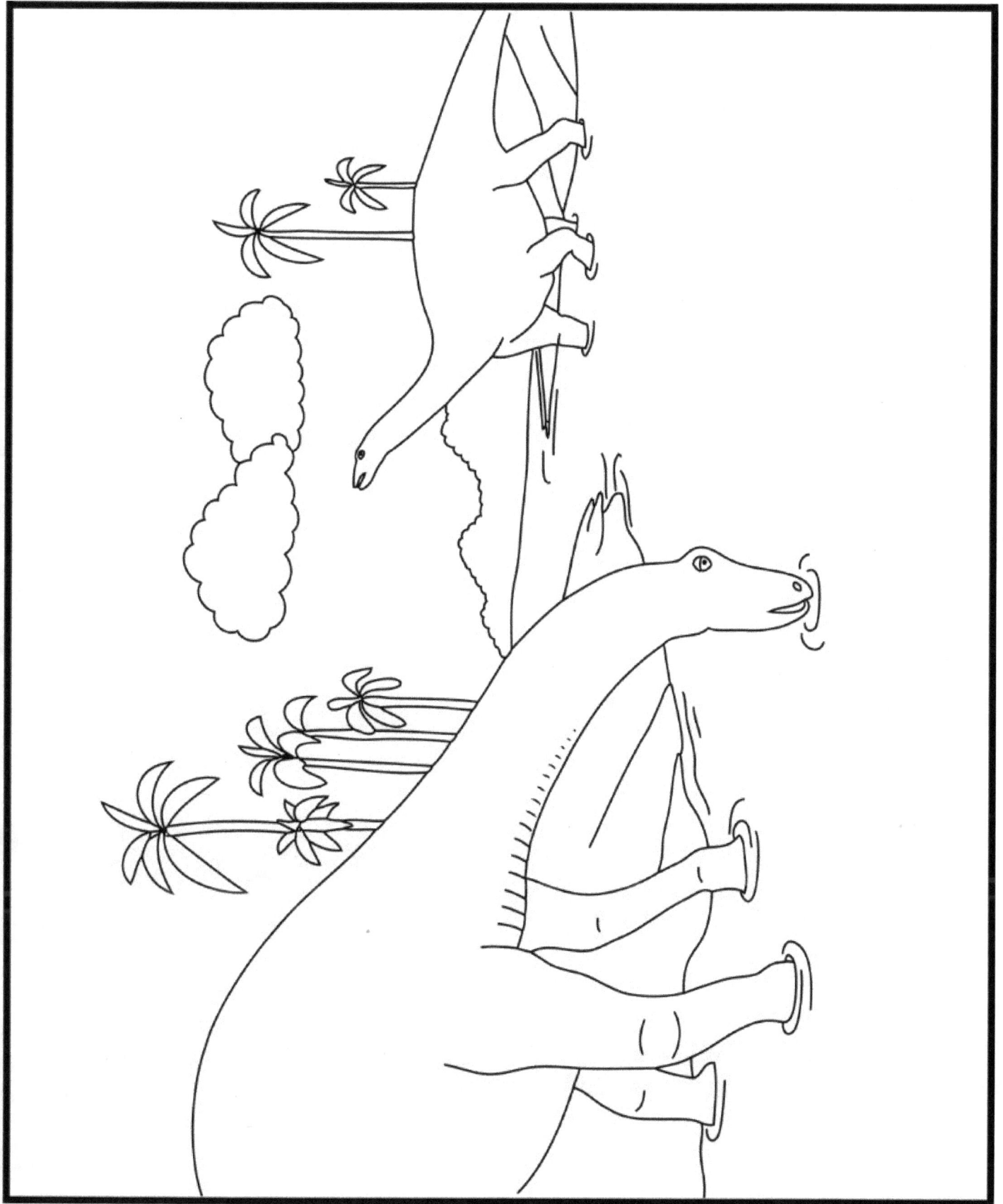

Draw The Dinosaur You Like Best

Draw A Dinosaur Standing Outside Where You Live…

Draw The Funniest Dinosaur You Can Think Of

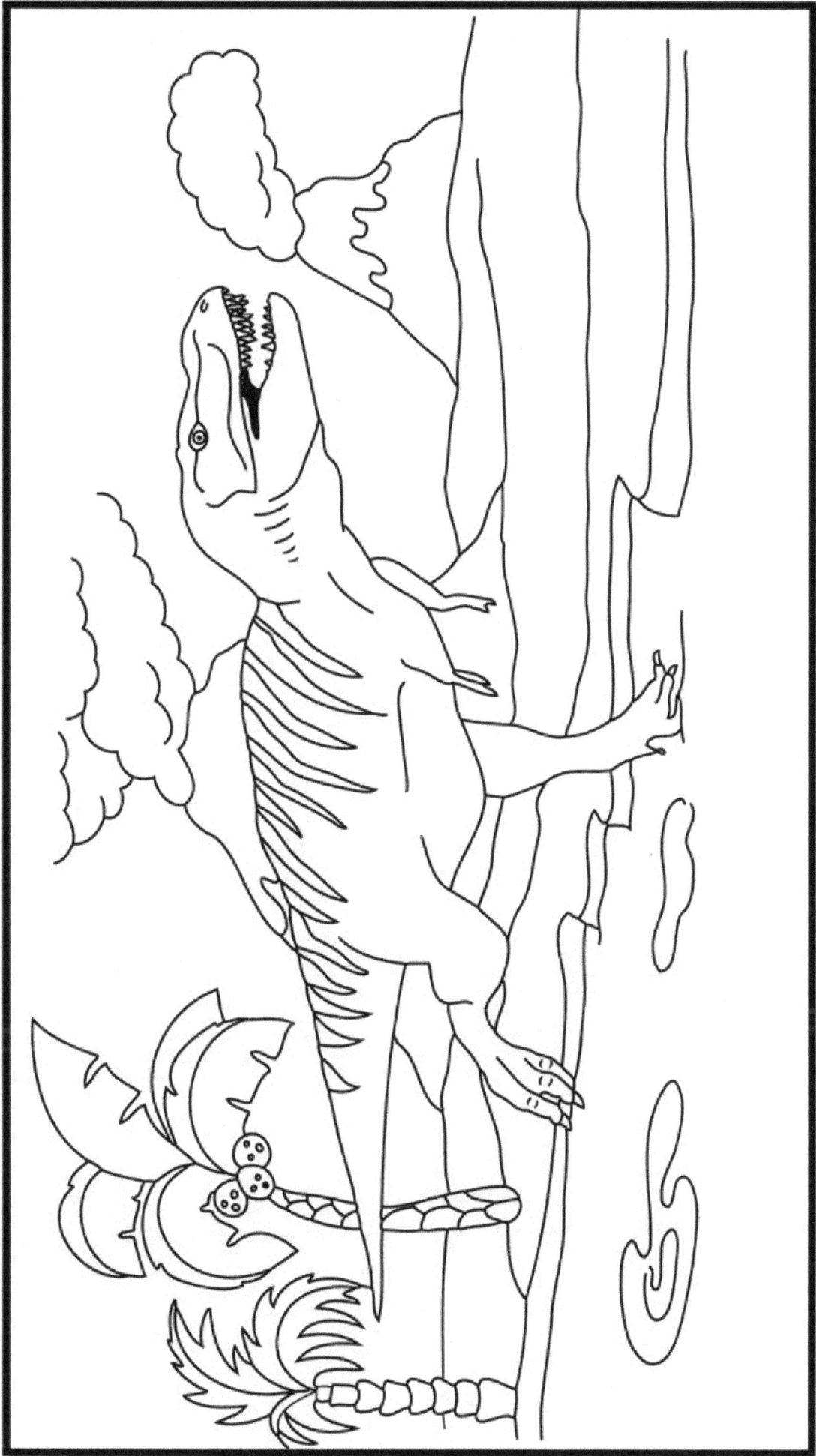

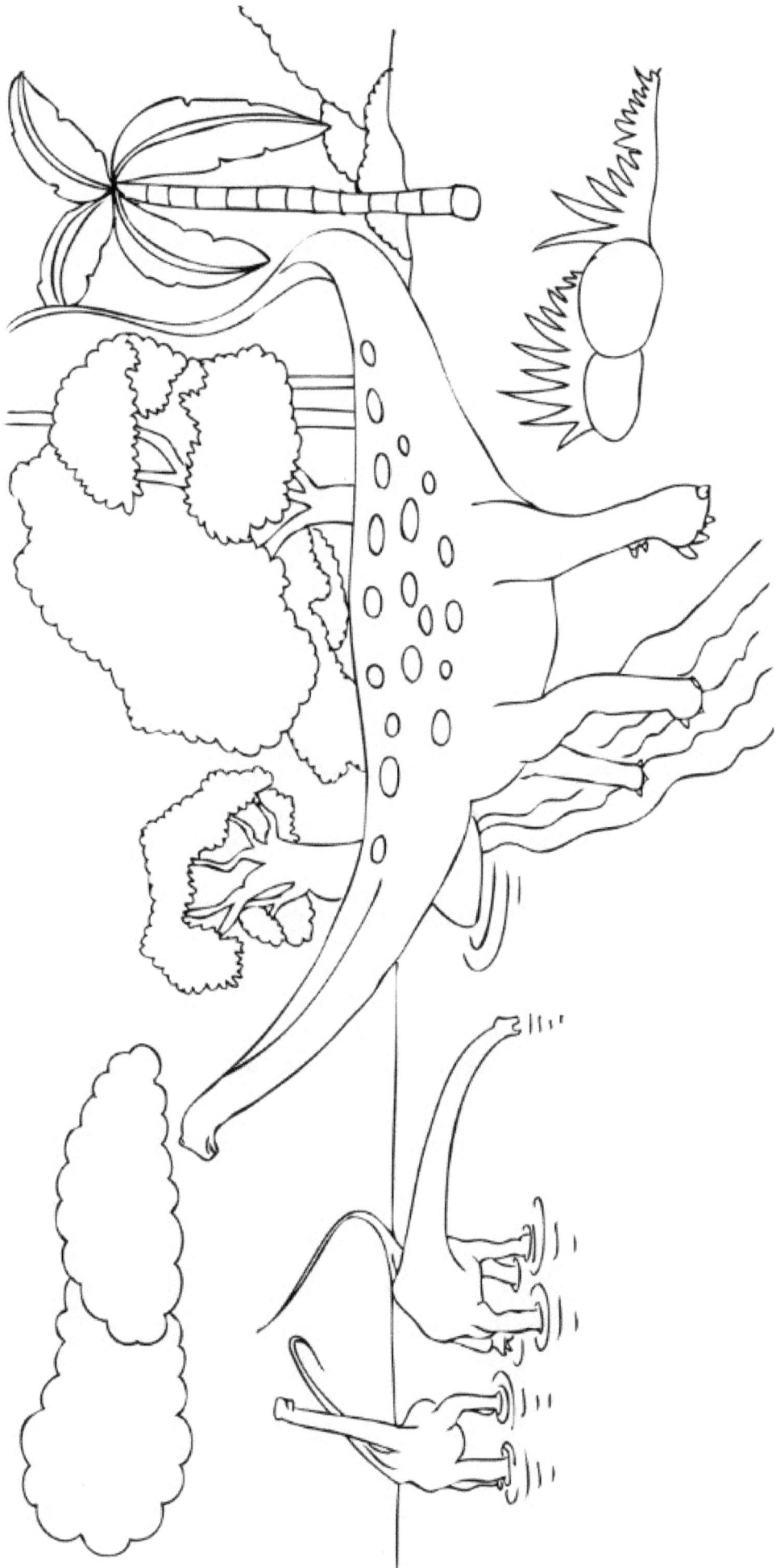

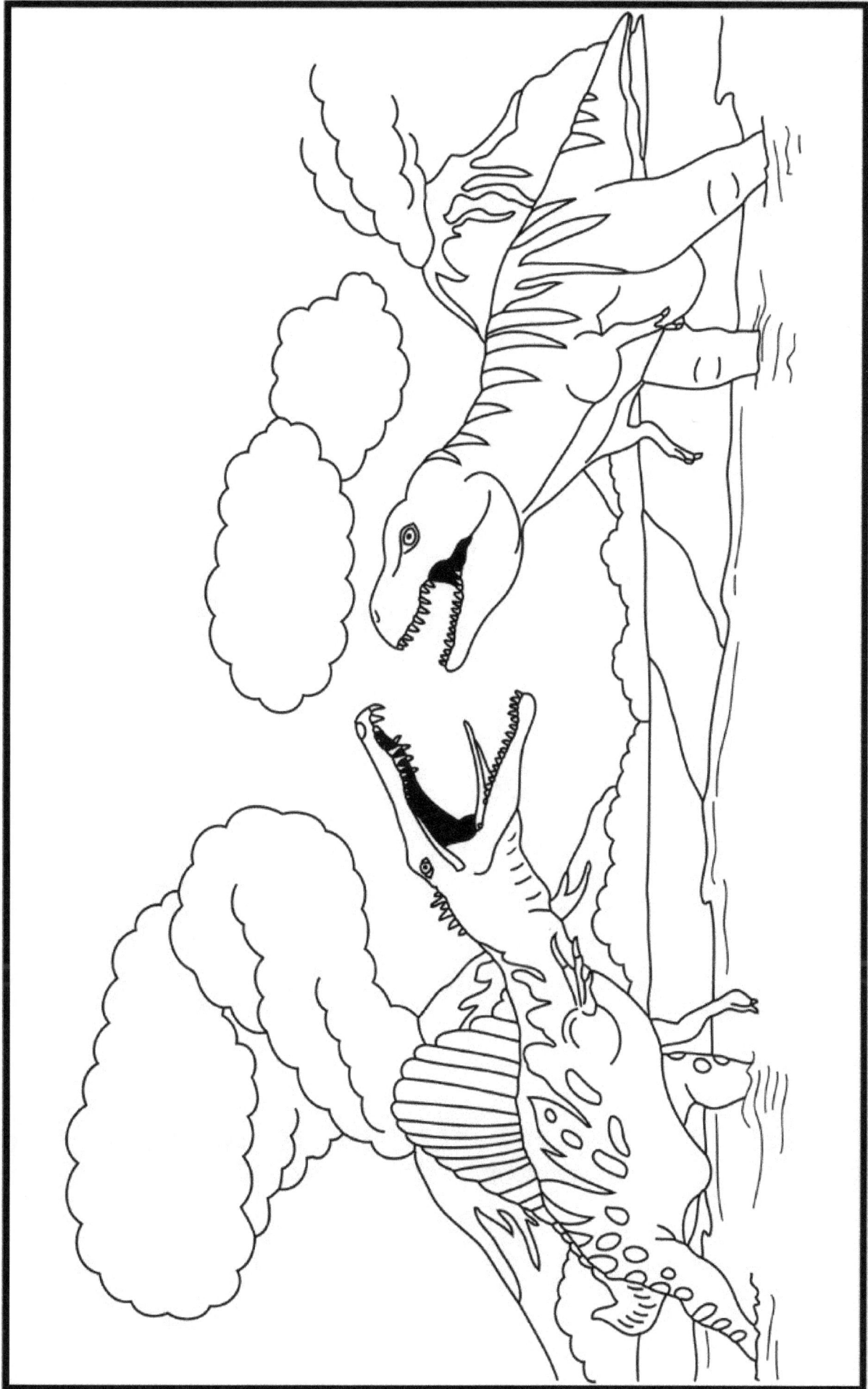

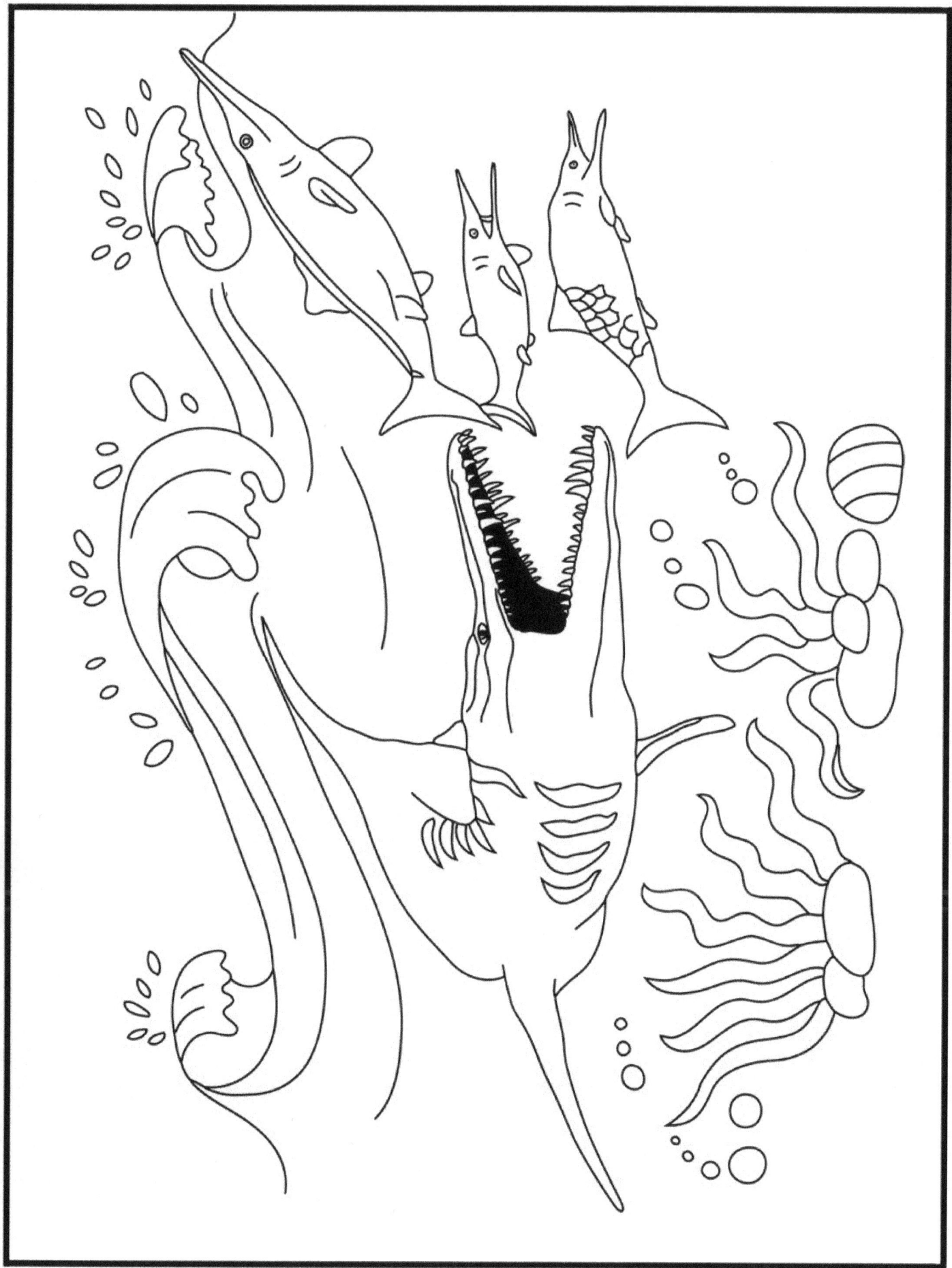

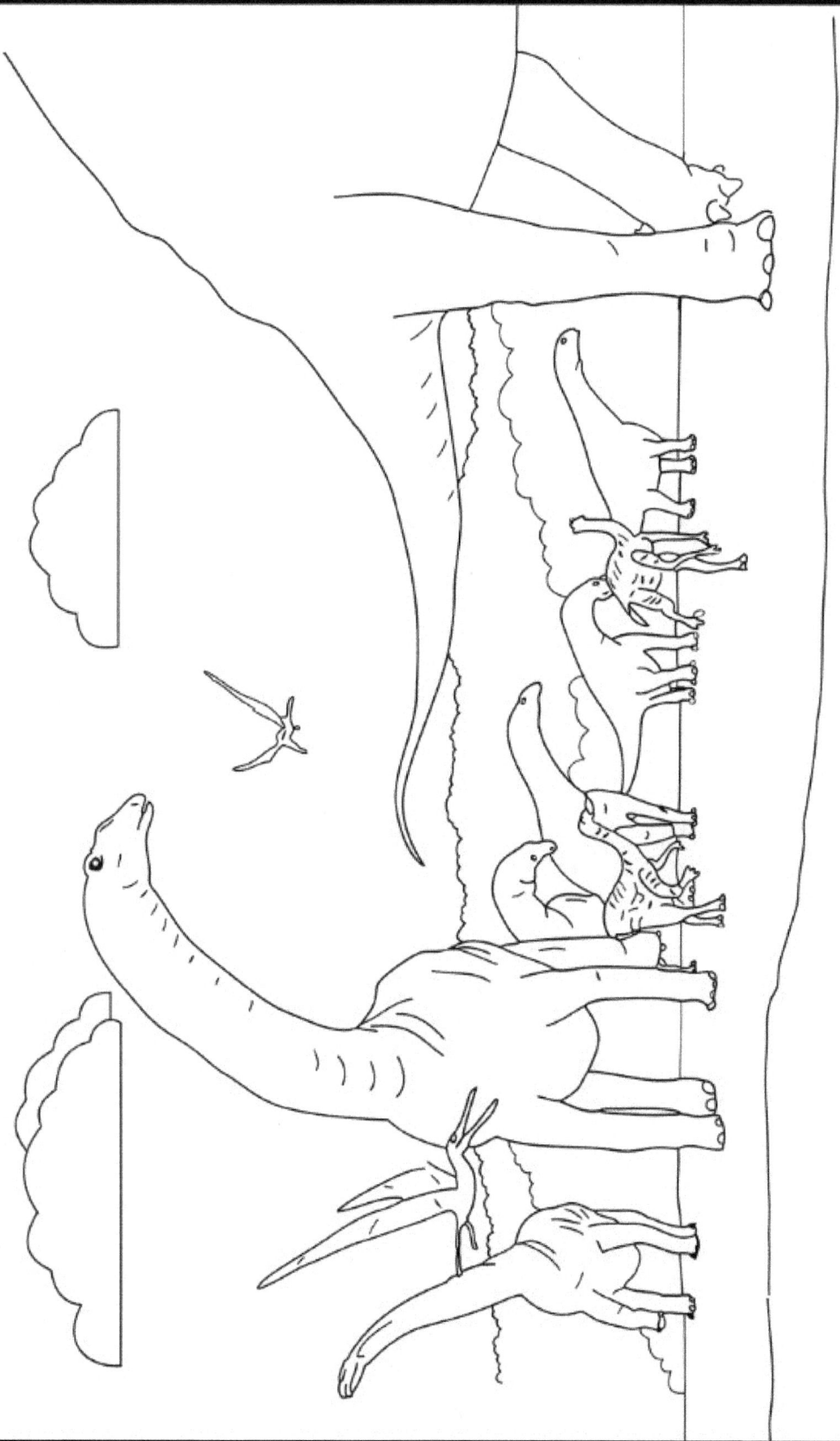

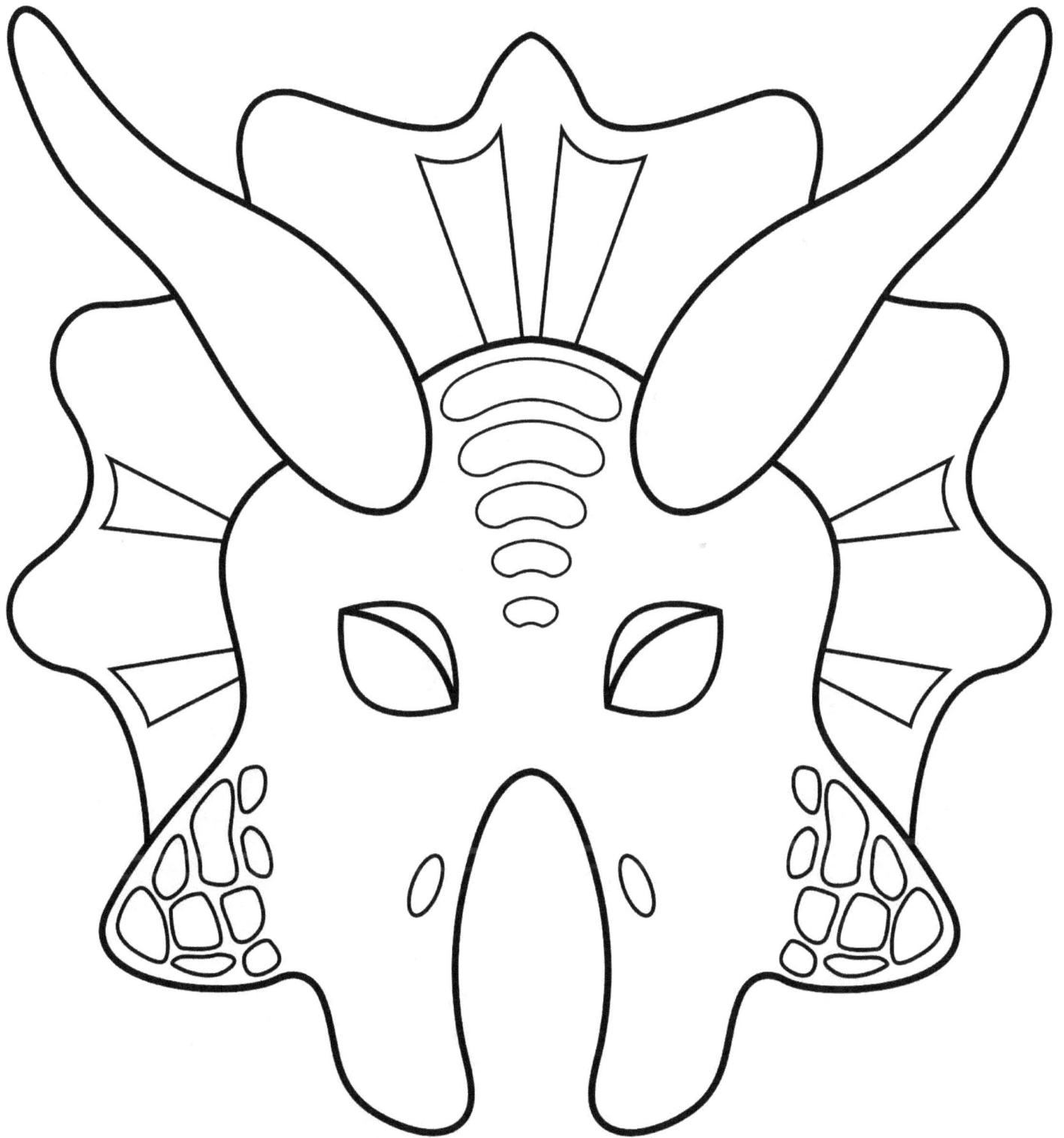

About Me

I have loved drawing from a very young age and now it is my pleasure to share with you some of my latest images.

My children love dinosaurs and these are some of the images I drew for them. I hope you enjoy coloring all the dinosaurs.

The benefits of coloring have been widely reported. It's great for children

- Helping to improve concentration
- Improving hand to eye coordination
- Practice holding writing tools, developing their tiny hand muscles
- Learning to focus on details
- Recognizing colors, shapes, patterns, shades
- Great way to relax and calm down
- Helps to improve handwriting
- Stimulates creativity
- And lots more…..
-

If you've enjoyed coloring these designs – Please can you help me?

Hopefully you've enjoyed coloring some or all of these images. If you have please, please, please can you take the time to share your thoughts and post a review on whatever site you purchased it from? It will be greatly appreciated and really help me – thank you.

MORE FREE COLORING IMAGES...

Would you like to color some or all of these images in again? Perhaps in different colors or styles. Now you can print out as many copies as you like. We'll send you every design in this book free.

Please just visit http://www.ColoringFans.com/roartoday

so we can send you all the designs today.

Thank you so much for purchasing this book. I hope you have many happy hours coloring in all the wonderful images. As an extra 'thank you' simply join our free club.

We'll send you all the designs as a pdf document so you can just print them off at home as many times as you like - you can even print them for your friends, please just mention us. Just don't upload them online, sell them or claim they are yours!

Plus we'll send you advance designs from our new coloring books for you to enjoy free. If you'd like to 'show off' your skills I'm also putting together a gallery of your achievements. Details included when you join free.

http://www.ColoringFans.com/roartoday Please visit today